The FRUIT OF THE SPIRIT

for little ones

Mandy Fender

The Fruit of the Spirit for Little Ones
Copyright 2022 Mandy Fender

https://www.shutterstock.com/image-vector/small-children-holding-big-fruits-cute-2063515631
https://www.shutterstock.com/image-vector/group-children-circle-funny-cartoon-character-1913400001
https://www.shutterstock.com/image-vector/colorful-bright-fruits-drawn-on-blue-1094489723

THIS BOOK BELONGS TO:

_____

But the fruit of the Spirit is love, joy, peace, patience, kindness, goodness, faithfulness, gentleness, self-control…
Galatians 5:22-23
(ESV)

THE
FRUIT
OF THE
SPIRIT
THAT GOD HAS GIVEN ME...

HELPS ME BE EVERYTHING I SHOULD BE.

The fruit of
LOVE
gives me strength from above to care and share.

The fruit of JOY makes me glad when I am feeling sad.

The fruit of **PEACE** helps me stay calm even when the day is long.

The fruit of

gives me

power to wait when things
seem late.

The fruit of

kindness

reminds me to be nice and kind to everyone I find.

The fruit of

goodness helps

me to be and do good as I

should.

The fruit of

gives me faith to grow and
helps me believe what I know.

The fruit of

gentleness

is really quite simple, it makes me gentle.

The fruit of

SELF-

CONTROL

helps me to be strong and to get along.

I am so thankful for the

fruit

of the spirit

God has given me and will use
it every day, and with
everyone I see.

SAY IT WITH ME! LOVE, JOY, PEACE, PATIENCE, KINDNESS, GOODNESS, FAITHFULNESS, GENTLENESS, AND SELF-CONTROL!

Dear Parents, Teachers, and Guardians,

Thank you so much for reading my book with your little ones! I pray that it was a blessing and helped teach the Fruit of the Spirit in a fun way! May the Lord's blessing and favor always be upon you and your children!

Many Blessings,
Mandy Fender

Made in United States
Troutdale, OR
02/27/2024

17982595R00024